MW00676944

For You, My Friend,
I Wish . . .

For You, My Friend, I Wish . . .

350 Kind, Funny, Wise, and Wonderful Wishes

Written and illustrated by
Lorraine Bodger

**Andrews McMeel
Publishing**

Kansas City

00 01 02 03 04 TWP 10 9 8 7 6 5 4 3 2 1

ISBN: 0-7407-0990-9

Library of Congress Catalog Card Number: 00-101319

Book design by Lisa Martin

Introduction

Wishing is about dreaming, about letting yourself imagine that the things you want can, indeed, happen. It's about the fun of playing "Wouldn't it be great if . . ." Wishing is a delicious pleasure—easy to do, infinite in variety, and it doesn't cost a cent. You need lots of good wishes, and these good wishes from your friend—350 of them—will boost your hope and optimism, inspire and stimulate you, offer you comfort, give you perspective. These wishes will make you laugh and help you keep your sense of humor during trying times. They may even nudge you toward smart decisions about your love affairs, your family, or your career. Wishes can do all that and more.

It's true that many wishes are simply wry and funny acknowledgments of life's little ironies (I wish I hadn't bumped into Heartthrob Harry on a horrible hair day), but slews of other wishes are coded messages about your larger goals. Sometimes it seems as if you can only tiptoe up to a big "I want" if you put it the form of a small "I wish." And it's a whole lot easier if a friend does it for you!

If you listen carefully to the wish your friend makes for you, something wonderful happens: You learn about your own aspirations (that's good) and then you see that you have choices (that's better). Your friend has put a wish out there on the table and you can say to yourself, Terrific, that's exactly what I want and I'm going after it. Or you can say, Hmm, maybe that's not quite the ticket—put that one on hold. Sometimes you'll say, That's a wonderful long-term wish, and I need to plan for it so I can achieve it. At other times you might say, Whoopee, I can do that right this minute! What am I waiting for? And always, always you can read and think about a dozen wishes—and do absolutely nothing more than indulge in the pleasure of fantasizing, dreaming, and letting your imagination lead you to places and ideas you've never before contemplated.

Good wishes are the most generous kind of expectations, and the friend who gives you this book has heartfelt and genuine expectations for you. She hopes, as I do, that all the wishes here—from the small, funny ones to the large, serious ones—will tickle your fancy and make you think.

What do you wish for yourself? Wish big, wish small, wish for today, and wish for tomorrow. And may all your wishes come true.

For You, My Friend, I Wish That . . .

You win the lottery. Big-time.

Your bathroom scale was off,
and you actually weigh five pounds
less than you thought you did.

The dinner you cook for your new
in-laws comes off without a hitch.

You're eating alone in a good
restaurant when a dreamboat asks
to share your table—and turns
out to be the love of your life.

The value of your investments
goes up and up and up.

It was only a rumor that they stopped
making your favorite mascara.

You're snug and warm inside when the blizzard starts.

Your air conditioner is working at peak performance
when the thermometer hits ninety-five.

The plumber arrives at exactly the
time he said he'd arrive.

You get the promotion you so richly deserve,
and the raise to go with it.

You have your umbrella
handy when the rain
comes pelting down.

Your computer never crashes.

But if it does, you don't lose
a single byte of data.

Last summer's clothes fit you
even better this summer.

You answer the quiz question correctly and win
an all-expenses-paid trip to Europe for two.

You find the house of your dreams the
first day you go out looking.

The dentist can take you right away
when you have a terrible toothache.

There's a tax refund for you when
you weren't expecting one.

There's just enough milk left in the
carton for your morning cup of coffee.

You decide that the glass is
half full instead of half empty.

Your significant other does his share
of the housework without being asked.

Your kids tell you they've gotten
tattoos—but they haven't.

A writer uses you as a character in her book.

Your car never breaks down on a
dark highway, miles from a service station.

❖

A traffic cop pulls you over to
tell you what a good driver you are.

❖

The director of the amateur theater group
begs you to take the starring role.

❖

When you accidentally leave your handbag in a taxicab,
the next passenger finds it, calls you, and delivers it
right to your door. And refuses any reward.

❖

You never lose your keys.

❖

You never lose a night's sleep.

The misty seafoam green you
chose for the living room walls turns
out to be exactly right.

You find your soul mate.

You learn to love working out.

You take the time to do
whatever makes you feel really good.
And you do it often.

On a cold night, someone warms the bed for you.

Another tourist in a foreign city mistakes
you for a native and asks you for directions.

Everything in your
garden comes up.

You're never disappointed in your friends,
and you never disappoint them, either.

You drive off for a spur-of-the-moment
weekend trip, and just when you despair of finding
a decent place to spend the night, you stumble
onto the world's most adorable country inn.

Every piece of modern technology you
purchase—portable phone, fax, laptop, VCR,
CD player, treadmill, food processor—works
perfectly from the moment you plug it in.

You decide, after months of waffling,
to cut your hair—and it looks great!

You get bumped from coach to first class.

You can take a day off
when you need a day off.

You marry someone who
loves to do home repair.

Just when you're feeling desperate
about your current job, the personnel
manager from another company calls to
ask if you're interested in a fantastic
position that's just opened up.

You notice the banana peel before
you have a chance to slip on it.

You find the right mentor.

You're browsing an antique show,
and you come across a complete service
of gorgeous old silverware engraved with
your initials, at a price you can afford.

❖

When the chocolate madness
comes over you, there's a bar of your
all-time favorite candy hiding in
the back of the freezer.

❖

You bump into your old boyfriend
when you've just had your hair done
and you're dressed to kill.

❖

The flowering trees in your yard
drop thousands of petals to make
a silky carpet for you to lie on.

There's never a line at the bank.

If it looks sensational on you, you buy two.

You reread your favorite novel,
and it's even better the second time.

You watch your favorite movie on videotape,
and it's just as good as the first time you saw it.

Someone spots your doodles and offers
you a cartoon strip in the local paper.

Someone spots your cartoon strip
in the local paper and offers
you national syndication.

When you sneak downstairs for a midnight snack,
there's a big piece of blueberry pie left.

The next ten videos you
rent are all winners.

You suddenly discover a hitherto
unknown ability to organize

your desk drawers

your closet

your kitchen

your life.

You give and get the little things
that make each day a pleasure:
a phone call, a pat on the back, a smile.

You get to take a cross-country
train trip in your own roomette.

For seven days in a row
you wake up in a good mood.

The moth you saw in the
living room loses his way before
he gets to your clothes closet.

One of your kids turns out to
love doing the laundry and takes
care of the wash every week.

Another of your kids turns out
to be a fantastic cook and makes
dinner every night.

The secretary of state gives you
a call to check out your opinions
on the latest world crisis.

You win the

tennis match

dance contest

three-legged race

bake-off

poetry slam.

Daylight saving time ended
last night, but you forgot to set the
clock back—so you can sleep
for another hour this morning.

You plan the
perfect wedding,
and it *is* perfect.

You never forget

your locker combination

your mother-in-law's first name

your ATM PIN

the code for your security system

where you left your car

how to undelete.

You figure out the thing you want
most in life and go after it.

You actually feel thankful at Thanksgiving.

Someone else changes the sheets this week.

You quit postponing that
long-delayed vacation, that weekend away,
that afternoon of free time.

※

You decide to stop being superstitious.

※

You never get embroiled in
office politics, but your office buddy
tells you all the juicy gossip anyway.

※

You make a list of why you should
and why you shouldn't, and the
shoulds come out ahead.

※

A really great gym opens near your office,
so you can work out on all those amazing
machines before you head home.

You find someone who adores
making love just the way you do.

❖

Your confidence, optimism, enthusiasm,
and idealism never fail you.

❖

The old timepiece you pluck from
a trunk in the attic turns out to be the rare
1933 Ingersoll Mickey Mouse pocket watch.

❖

At least once in your life you get to stay
in a four-star deluxe hotel with all the amenities,
including major amounts of room service.

❖

You learn the art of being a good listener,
and you find a good listener to listen to you, too.

Your life has sweetness:
fragrant roses, lilies, and freesia;
chocolate cookies; vanilla milkshakes; the kindness
of a dear friend; love notes; a beautifully wrapped
gift; a jar of thyme honey; a new baby.

❖

Your life has spice:
cinnamon sticks tied with plaid ribbon;
steak au poivre; a bowl of pungent potpourri;
a racy novel; mulled wine; chicken curry
with chutney; an exciting new lover.

❖

Your life has zest:
a big glass of fresh lemonade; an exhilarating
ride on a roller coaster; a bracing swim in a
mountain pool; ice-cold champagne; fresh pine
boughs for decorating the house; apple picking
on a crisp autumn afternoon; ocean spray.

Your life has comfort:
soft pillows for your bed; fuzzy slippers;
good walking shoes; a fireplace; hot cocoa with
marshmallows; a great armchair and a great
desk chair; big closets; rice pudding; a warm coat.

You become known as an agent of positive change.

There's always someone to
scratch your back when it itches.

When you're summoned
to jury duty, you're put on an interesting
case that's over quickly.

You turn out to have a flair for public speaking and
become an incredible asset to your company.

An exotic island shimmers
on your horizon, and you go there
with your one-and-only.

Instead of waiting around for
Prince Charming to come along and
rescue you, you go out and rescue yourself!

You have a great Chinese meal—in China.

You develop a talent for

making cookies

making baste

making money

making love.

You get to meet the person you've
always admired from afar.

You always feel safe, secure, and cared for.

A massage therapist with magic
fingers works out all your kinks.

You travel to the places you've
fantasized about, from the Grand Canyon
to the Eiffel Tower, the plains of the
Serengeti to the Great Wall of China.

At the next wedding you attend,
you catch the bouquet.

You live long enough to see the first
female president of the United States.

When asked for your opinion at the
important meeting, you give it clearly,
logically, and winningly.

Your

a) mother

b) boyfriend

c) best friend

d) all of the above

don't freak out when you pierce
your ears with a few more holes.

❖

You turn one room of your home into
a place that suits you to a tee: a quiet room
for relaxing, an office for writing, a workout room
full of equipment, a music room with a sound system,
a sewing room with plenty of storage.

❖

Each day you take time for yourself,
even if it's just half an hour.

The CD you make on a lark
soars right off the charts.

✥

Your independent film, financed by
friends and family, wins prizes at film festivals.

✥

At least once, you have an epiphany.

✥

You check off every item of importance
on your to-do list and ignore the rest.

✥

You're invited to an incredibly
glam party for New Year's Eve.

✥

You do so many good works that they
give a testimonial dinner in your honor.

On a lazy Sunday morning,
your honey takes you out
for a fabulous brunch.

When life—in the form of a lover
or a friend—is disappointing, you take
whatever lesson there is to be learned and
move on. It can be done, and you can do it.

You always have a close-knit group of
friends to support you through thick and thin.

You treasure your memories—in handsome
photo albums and scrapbooks.

You have a nice, comfortable nest egg.

Just once, you get enough canapés at a cocktail party.

You never lose your sense of humor.

At the big dance you win the door prize.

At the county fair you win the blue ribbon.

At the raffle you have the winning ticket.

You take control of your life
when you need to, and the rest of the
time you relax and enjoy the ride.

Your clever hunches are always right,
and your fearful trepidations are always wrong.

A really great little café—with perfect
espresso, cappuccino, and latte—opens
right down the block from you.

Your fairy godmother takes
you on a mad shopping spree
at your favorite boutique.

❖

The pantry holds an unlimited
supply of your favorite munchies.

❖

None of your love goes unrequited.

❖

You write a list of ten goals
and make them happen, one by one.

❖

You feel comfortable asking for
a favor—and granting one, too.

❖

You find more time for fun.

At the end of a long day,
your feet don't hurt.

∴

The feng shui of your home
is just what it should be.

∴

You take a ten-minute break:
one turn around the block,
a retreat to privacy (lock that door!),
a catnap, a brief meditation,
a long daydream.

∴

You rediscover the pleasure of letter writing.

∴

You and your sweetheart
drive to a great necking spot,
and smooch till your lips are sore.

When you need a brief respite,
you escape to nature:
a mountain trail, bird sanctuary,
seashore, orchard, waterfall, desert.

You learn to shrug off your mistakes
and take your setbacks less seriously.

You learn to set priorities. Life is short.

You learn to compromise,
but only when necessary.

You join Packrats Anonymous
and get rid of all the useless stuff
that's crowding you out of your home.

You take a course in
financial planning and find out
your strategies are right on target.

Your boss makes a special trip down
the hall to your office to tell you what
a good job you're doing.

Your dinner parties become
famous for sensational food and
stimulating conversation.

The airline didn't really
lose your luggage.

But if it did, your makeup
is in your carry-on bag.

You find a satisfying way to let off steam:
singing at the top of your voice,
roller-blading full out,
punching a pillow,
jitterbugging till your legs fold.

If the path you've chosen is marriage,
you have a long and happy one.

You're never tempted to listen to people
who don't have your best interests at heart.

You choose a political or social issue
close to your heart, and work to resolve it.

You find the best way to
balance love and work.

You go to the
Wild Animal Park.

You get an extra phone line
so your friends can reach you when
your teenagers are yakking endlessly.

When you send your kids to summer camp,
they love it so much that you don't have
to feel guilty for enjoying their absence.

You spend July and August
working with a summer repertory
theater that puts on plays and
musicals at a posh resort.

You write a best-seller,
or at least you try.

You saved the very first Barbie
you ever had, and now you can
sell her and send your kids to
college on the proceeds.

·:·

On Thanksgiving your warm,
delicious-smelling kitchen is full
of happy family members
preparing a gigantic feast.

·:·

Someone else ties up
the stack of newspapers and
takes out the garbage.

·:·

There's a hot, fragrant bubble bath
waiting for you when you arrive
home after a tough day.

Tomorrow you wake up completely
content with your hips and thighs.

❖

You treat yourself to an evening
of reminiscing with your oldest friend,
wherever she may be. Get together
in person, by phone, or by e-mail.

❖

You have an active fantasy life and
the energy to indulge at least some of it.
Be daring (but be safe).

❖

The sun shines on the day
of your big presentation, so you don't
ruin your best suede shoes in the rain.

You get to drive, at least once,

a fire engine

a Ferrari

a motorcycle

a vintage Caddy.

At least once a week you can
oversleep without dire consequences.

You don't hesitate to walk out
of a dumb, obnoxious movie.

But if you love the movie,
you sit through it twice.

You think of the perfect person
to help you solve that intractable
problem, and she does.

You and your partner decide that yours
is the greatest love story every told.

You outgrow your fears.

Your creative juices always flow freely.

Your spelling miraculously improves.

You go to your high school reunion
and (surprise!) it's fun.

There's an endless supply of
good books for you to read.

You never break

your favorite knickknack

your living room window

your word

your heart.

❖

If you run for school board,
president of your club, city council,
or even mayor—you win!

❖

The dry cleaner does you the favor
of ruining that pair of pants you've always hated,
and offers to pay for them, too.

❖

There's always enough hot water.

Your search engine leads you
where you want to go.

You give yourself permission
to do something you enjoy even though
you're not very good at it.

You give yourself more mental or physical
room in which to grow and develop.

You take a week off in another
town, with time to explore, to eat new
foods, to browse and shop, to visit
museums and local sights, to forget
your real life for a little while.

You eat right and feel great because of it.

You take a little nap, and your
true love wakes you with a kiss.

⁕

Eureka! You find the perfect apartment
at a monthly rent you can easily afford.

⁕

You have a closet full of clothes
you love, so you never say
"I have nothing to wear!"

⁕

Thought becomes action,
and you start that business you've
been mulling for months or years.

⁕

You have a celebration whenever
you achieve a goal that's important to you.

Your letter to the editor gets printed
and changes a few minds.

You take a warm-weather
vacation during the icy depths of
winter, and a cold-weather vacation
when it's too hot to think straight.

Your adult-onset allergy doesn't
involve anything you really love . . .
like chocolate . . . or garlic . . . or cashmere.

You give yourself permission
to waste a little time.

You get credit for what you've truly earned.

At the end of each day,
your home is a haven of peace.

You always know the
right thing to say.

❖

You never spill red wine
on your white jeans.

❖

It takes only half the time you thought
it would take to clear your desk.

❖

You get in on the ground
floor of the next Microsoft.

❖

If you get stuck in an elevator,
the only other occupant is either
an extremely reassuring grandmother
or a divinely attractive guy.

When you apply for a new job,
you receive glowing recommendations
from your former employers.

❖

The scary creaks you hear in
the middle of the night are nothing
more than the house settling.

❖

Your grandchildren love hanging
out with you, and vice versa.

❖

Your oldest, deepest, most
meaningful friendships last forever.

❖

When you go on vacation, you remember
to pack everything you meant to pack.

You feel free to order
two desserts instead of one.

If you get stuck in traffic,
your favorite talk show is on the radio.

❖

You recapture memories
that give you joy.

❖

You venture beyond a paint-by-numbers
life and find the unconventional.

❖

You hit the road for a couple of
weeks to sample all those delicious regional
specialties you've been hearing about.

❖

Your kids never get cavities
and don't need braces.

There's a hammock slung between
two beautiful old trees, a tall glass of
something good to drink, and a long
summer afternoon for you to enjoy them.

❖

You have an actual, real, authentic
conversation with your adolescent.

❖

Someone makes hot oatmeal
for you on a winter morning.

❖

Magically, there's clean
underwear even though you didn't
have time to do the laundry.

❖

Your sweetie volunteers to massage
your neck whenever it's stiff.

You accomplish your goals—
daily, weekly, yearly, lifelong.

You and your partner take
the honeymoon trip you couldn't afford
to take when you got married.

You never allow unimportant little
disagreements to turn into big fights.

You take advantage of opportunities
whenever they occur.

Your alumni magazine does
a big article about you.

Order miraculously descends
over your life.

❖

You learn the joys of
intimate friendship.

❖

Your dreams come true.

❖

You're never bored.

❖

You get through to tech
support whenever you want,
without being put on hold.

❖

You don't catch the flu this winter.

The box of love letters
you thought you lost during
your last move turns up safe and
sound after your next move.

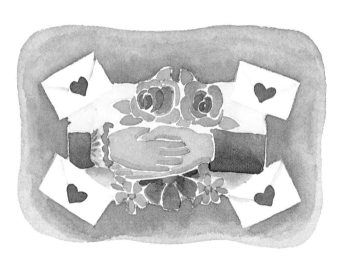

Friends call with great plans for the
weekend just when you thought you had
nothing to do on Saturday and Sunday.

You feel that amazing, electric
jolt of attraction to someone you
never even expected to like.

In this age of jeans, you
get to wear a glamorous evening
gown at least once.

Before the winter sets in,
you act like a squirrel and stock your
pantry with goodies (jars of jam, tins of
cookies, cans of cashews) for treats
on snowbound nights.

If you need them, you find you
have vast reserves of inner strength.

If you're unexpectedly called upon
to make a toast or a speech, the perfect
words come to you instantly.

You celebrate each season by
enjoying its special activities,
holidays, and seasonal foods.

Someone sends you
a care package.

Your life is as exciting as your
favorite romance novel.

You never miss out on anything
you really want to do.

Your candidate wins by a landslide.

Your kids' favorite
baby-sitter never cancels.

When someone you love
is in need of comfort,
you're there for her.

You feel free to turn off
the phone and retire from the
world for a little while.

You have enough pockets.

❖

You have enough electrical outlets.

❖

Unexpectedly, you receive
a month of free cable TV.

❖

An interesting-looking man
catches your eye and sends a drink to
your table; you meet and fall in love.

❖

You discover the fragrance
that suits you perfectly.

❖

Your checkbook always balances.

You volunteer at your local
public radio station and wind up
with a show of your own.

✦

There's a cold beer waiting
in the fridge when you come in
from plowing the north forty.

✦

Your immediate family moves
closer—or farther away.

✦

The squeaky door, leaky faucet,
and sticky drawer mysteriously fix themselves.

✦

Your children learn to play quietly,
so you can take a breather.

A friend just happens to offer you and your family her beach house for the two weeks that just happen to be your vacation.

Your car insurance
covers the entire repair.

❖

You plan a fun day with your
best friend: manicures, mud packs,
a movie, and a lavish dinner at
a hip new restaurant.

❖

You discover the perfect
a) bathing suit (very flattering)
b) winter boots (warm and waterproof)
c) undies (no panty line)
d) jeans (they fit!)
e) all of the above

❖

You come home one afternoon
to find that an elf has cleared
all the junk out of your garage.

When you've cried a river,
your most reliable friend reminds
you that things will get better.
Believe her. They will.

⋅⋅⋅

You give yourself an
old-fashioned treat: a sledding party,
a picnic, a moonlit evening of
ice skating, a campfire with marshmallows
and ghost stories.

⋅⋅⋅

You're blessed with perfect timing:
The check comes on the correct date.
The baby arrives when she's supposed to.
The closing happens on schedule.
Your spouse never keeps you waiting.

You ditch those postholiday
extra pounds before they
become permanent.

❖

You never receive junk
faxes or junk e-mails.

❖

Luck is with you: You find
the perfect couch in a marvelous
color at the right price.

❖

You think you did a good
job of raising your children—
and they agree with you.

❖

You turn a new friend into an old one.

You experience the lightened
heart that comes from unburdening
yourself to a trustworthy friend.

After a three-week vacation,
you look so rested that everyone
thinks you had a face-lift.

This year your true love
gives you a partridge in a pear tree
and all the other delights of Christmas.

They invent a completely self-cleaning
litter box for your cat.

You learn to accept change, and love it.

Your boss sends you flowers
to thank you for your excellent
work on the latest big project.

You take an inspiring trip into
the past to find your roots,
wherever they may be.

✦

One day you overhear a
conversation in the foreign language
you've been studying—and you
understand every word of it!

✦

You grant yourself a few hours
in an oasis, any place you consider
a refreshing spot in the desert:
a café, a library, a fabric store,
a greenmarket, an art gallery.

✦

When the lights go out, your flashlight
works and the candles are handy.

You and your partner decide,
ten years after the wedding,
that you still enjoy each other's company.
Treasure the moment.

You have a mosquito-free summer.

You bring peace to your marriage
with the aid of his-and-hers technology:
two televisions, two computers, two phone lines,
and two answering machines.

Your parents stop criticizing you.
And you stop criticizing them.

Your shoes don't pinch.

On Valentine's Day you receive
a big box of assorted chocolates
with all your favorite fillings.

You discover a natural ability you
didn't even know you had.

Your great-aunt Minnie
lives to a happy old age, and then
leaves you an unexpected legacy
of oodles of cash.

You find the calm in
the eye of the storm.

You graduate from cyber-dating
to real dating, but only when you're ready.

You land a great job in Europe
and get to travel all over the Continent
on your weekends and vacations.

You receive a baker's dozen
passionate kisses under the mistletoe.

There's a stack of presents
under the tree and a Christmas stocking
full of goodies—all for you.

The Perfect Doughnut,
Penultimate Chili Dog,
or World's Best Apple Pie
turns up right in your hometown.

You develop a green thumb,
indoors and out.

You learn to say no and
you learn to say yes.

You have élan, panache, and savoir faire.

You always try to behave
in a way that gets you exactly
what you want.

You have hilarious nights out
with your friends and quiet nights
in with your beloved.

When you take the car in
for its 100,000-mile checkup,
it's in tip-top condition.

You celebrate your golden
wedding anniversary.

On your next flight there's no
one in the seat beside you
(so you can stretch out) or there's
someone wonderful in the seat
beside you (so you can flirt).

You accentuate the positive and
eliminate the negative.

Your nail polish never chips.

The world can be shaped to your taste:
Move the furniture around.
Change the color of the walls.
Buy new slipcovers.
Get rid of all the things
you don't absolutely love.

Someone else washes
the salad greens.

You treat yourself to a sneak-away
afternoon at the movies, with popcorn and soda
and any other kid food you feel like having.

※

Your friends adore you
just the way you are.

※

You nurture your curiosity.

※

You frolic in a mountain pool with
a waterfall and let the cascade of clear water
wash your everyday worries away.

※

Fortunately, you have smart kids
who listen to your good advice and
tactfully ignore your bad advice.

You have appreciation for the
easygoing people in your life and patience
for the more difficult ones.

❖

You turn off the TV in favor of playing
board games with your family.

❖

You have a secret crush on
someone—and discover that he has
a secret crush on you, too.

❖

You change careers whenever
you feel the need to.

❖

Instead of resenting them,
you enjoy the surprises in your life.

Rather than going out, you cozy
into a lazy evening by the fire, with plenty
of good bread, cheese, and wine.

❖

You have privacy when you want it
and good company the rest of the time.

❖

You and your sanity survive
your children's teenage years.

❖

If you're running too fast, you slow down—and
if you're lagging behind, you get a move on!

❖

You and your beloved stumble upon a
heavenly beach in a secluded cove surrounded
by gorgeous trees and fragrant flowers.

You remember to bring
an extra roll of film.

You're the most popular kid

on the block

in your class

in the office.

Your sound system sounds terrific.

You're invited to a power lunch.

On your fifteenth anniversary,
your wedding dress still fits.

You never sit by the phone waiting
for that special someone to call.
Either call him yourself, or get out
and meet a new guy.

❖

You and your mate cultivate
a relationship in which you can tell each
other your needs, and try to fulfill them.

❖

The problem-du-jour can be
solved easily by hiring the right pro:
dog walker, tailor, career counselor,
nutritionist, housekeeper, math coach.

❖

Your company decides to provide
excellent child care on the premises.

They invent an alarm clock that
wakes you gently and soothingly.

When you've scheduled a date
with someone you don't really
want to see, she cancels first.

❖

Against all odds, you accomplish the one thing
you've always wanted to achieve.

❖

You spend a day without burdens:
Leave your handbag, tote bag,
backpack, attaché case, and
shopping bags at home.

❖

There's a hot fudge sundae waiting
for you whenever you want it.

❖

You inspire loyalty.

You have friends of all ages.

You stop being too hard on yourself.
Give yourself the same break you'd
give to your best friend.

Your work schedule can be
arranged to avoid the morning
and evening rush hours.

Your love of reading (or chamber
music or volleyball) leads you to
like-minded people, and bingo!
you have community.

Congratulations! You stick to your
diet until you reach your goal.

Your kids have wonderful teachers.

❖

Your vacations always live up
to your expectations.

❖

There's an excellent bottle
of champagne cooling in the ice bucket,
and you know just the right
person to share it with.

❖

You challenge yourself often,
and you do it in a positive way that
keeps you going back for more.

❖

You're proud of your parents,
and they are proud of you.

Friends who make you feel guilty
are friends you decide to do without.

❖

You keep your Rolodex up to date.

❖

You always have a spare pair of panty hose.

❖

You have something delightful
to look forward to and something
heartwarming to look back on.

❖

You and your partner indulge yourselves:
Take a shower together or go skinny-dipping.
Cuddle up in front of a fire, indoors or out.
Take a midnight stroll in summer or winter.
Stay in bed all day.

There's a shoulder to cry on
whenever you need it.

❖

You experience the trust between lovers
that allows confidence and confidences.

❖

You find time to sit and
watch the world go by.

❖

You have everything you deeply desire.